fox woman get out!

fox woman get out!
INDIA LENA GONZÁLEZ

Foreword by Aracelis Girmay

New Poets of America Series, No. 50

BOA EDITIONS, LTD. ✷ ROCHESTER, NY ✷ 2023

First Edition
22 23 24 25 7 6 5 4 3 2 1

For information about permission to reuse any material from this book, please contact The Permissions Company at www.permissionscompany.com or e-mail permdude@gmail.com.

Publications by BOA Editions, Ltd.—a not-for-profit corporation under section 501 (c) (3) of the United States Internal Revenue Code—are made possible with funds from a variety of sources, including public funds from the Literature Program of the National Endowment for the Arts; the New York State Council on the Arts, a state agency; and the County of Monroe, NY. Private funding sources include the Max and Marian Farash Charitable Foundation; the Mary S. Mulligan Charitable Trust; the Rochester Area Community Foundation; the Ames-Amzalak Memorial Trust in memory of Henry Ames, Semon Amzalak, and Dan Amzalak; the LGBT Fund of Greater Rochester; and contributions from many individuals nationwide. See Colophon on page 98 for special individual acknowledgments.

Cover Art & Design: Sandy Knight
Interior Design and Composition: Michelle Dashevsky
BOA Logo: Mirko

BOA Editions books are available electronically through BookShare, an online distributor offering Large-Print, Braille, Multimedia Audio Book, and Dyslexic formats, as well as through e-readers that feature text to speech capabilities.

Cataloging-in-Publication Data is available from the Library of Congress.

BOA Editions, Ltd.
250 North Goodman Street, Suite 306
Rochester, NY 14607
www.boaeditions.org
A. Poulin, Jr., Founder (1938-1996)

*for those of us who are small and
lost our baby hairs in the fire*

CONTENTS

//   \\

||| ||

«« ««

afterwor(l)d

let me grow this spirit mouth (alas   )

FOREWORD

We have been invited to read. We have been invited to carry—in the arms of our own time(s)—the poet's formidable fight to protect her own vastness. She warns:

what shall i think i know well enough to call its name?

And:

if you are not careful   you can pay too much attention to one form
    & then you die without that sequoia making itself known
taking real root within you

I think of Cauleen Smith's gorgeous orange banners sewn with the velvet, final words of Alice Coltrane's *A Monument Eternal*: "At dawn, sit at the feet of action. At noon, be at the hand of might. At eventide be so big that sky will learn sky."

And so here is this book, this physical, spatial experience through which we readers might move, surrounded by material and memory, poems which read as portraits riven with multiple exposures. Accepting this invitation to read, we arrive with our own intricate possibilities and relationships, and in this way perhaps help India Lena to further disperse the energies of her many lives into the atmospheres that we, ourselves, move through and are. ("At eventide be so big that sky will learn sky.") In "C o N T I n e n T A L" she writes:

dear reader(s), i am assuming you are lost now
    you do not believe in such tiny sparks of divinity
  & yet, a couple of you must (not all third eyes can be easily ulcerated)

in a past life i was kublai khan, a whole tectonic plate
    i cannot make this up

And in "desert room #3 (el rey court)" she writes:

       in my head the italian director is preaching to me & twin
he says "go back to your elders & ask them about the plants."
          i want to say:
      "WHAT PLANTS?
       WHERE ARE MY ELDERS?
FIND THEM. BRING ME BACK MY INFORMATION."

We follow the capacious vision of the fox woman as she conjures language(s)
urgent, lamenting, fierce, and flickering enough to carry her multiplicities.
To me, what India Lena González has made is an exquisite beyond—a text/
revelation/performance/sounding that touches in me Jayne Cortez and Ntozake
Shange and Amiri Baraka to name a few, but is also so idiosyncratically
possessed by her own routes and people (plants, foxes, grandmothers, trees…).
I have not heard it before, this happening, which, to me, tries for an unending
sound. As she writes it: "let me grow this spirit mouth   (alas)".

::

aracelis girmay
brooklyn, ny
2023

we n' de ya ho

PART I

i am   sour meat   distressed birthmark

i utter your name *big mother* &   fry bread does not fall

    on my head   i go to pine ridge   rez &   they do not

applaud   no standing ||| o || i climb branches
        with their lakota children

                            bake apple pies out of plain dirt

        (bless us)

                    they take me to their newly departed cat   & do not cry

but the stench of it

        O UNCLE BUBBA UNCLE BUBBA WITH YOUR GLASS EYE

                    their father through screen door does not

        look at me   please

i shake their hands &   //   the earth will not rub off
                            on me \

    i buy a bone necklace   parade around the gas station

            linger at the counter begging for my name

            i force tiny indents into bottles   damn wasi'chu
        with / many \ teeth

they send me back up to the top   ««   sour meat   ««   distressed birthmark

        O UNCLE BUBBA UNCLE BUBBA

tell me about your hair   big mother // LENA \\ great grand mother

        they look at mine & say   i am in mourning

relentless mourning

       because   my hair hasn't gotten   to where   it's   trying to get to
  yet
                when i look back   lena   you're such real
cherokee

  you are not here

                              this woman
                              is a woman
                              no longer

PART II

LOOK AT MY HORSE EATIN' SAND

i'm talkin'   open-mouthed-windows
                                   & everyone damp inside

i'm talkin'   JASON MOMOA starin' straight outta
          my tv screen

            twin & i study his hands
          we love his hands
            & all the things he can do with them   shoot   he can
shoot   paint real good

          NOW THAT'S A MAN THAT'S A MAN THAT'S A MAN

                    SO BIG MUTHER   GUESS WHAT   !!!
        them blanquitas was staring at us
                    again with their pale hair &
      puritanical eyes
                                    like who was i
                    because they were real reservation
                                        government cheese

            new studies show that more   white || people
        claim cherokee   *to authenticate their american-ness*

            same old same old

                        BIG MUTHER why
        didn't you teach mama   how to   crouch   down | real | low | dance
for
them
        BIG THIGH MUSCLES ???

      i know a thing or two
                about stuffin' insulation in
          trailers for seasonal comfort

                                i know hikes where father
                                        pretends to fall off a cliff &
                        this never bothered us

                                BUT   BIG MUTHER i need you to talk
        about your medicine father
        (i need his salve)

& PLEASE THIS TIME
        FOR THE RECORD

        you understand   i'm sure
                        that sometimes a woman needs
something   someone
        to hurl herself up against

                                & RICHARD OAKES why'd you have to go
        & wear that
                        oatmeal turtleneck sweater   you got me & twin
over here sweatin'
        at the very sight of you

        BIG MUTHERRR.   LENA.   I'M BACK NOW.   & & & is it true?

                is it true that you came to my mother in a
                dream many deaths before i set in her bod-
                y? that you told her to name me INDIA L-
                ENA? is it because you knew i needed it?
                that twin was the real revolutionary? all red
                face & feathers growin' up her back? that s-
                he would show up at wounded knee, no wasi'-
                chu in sight & start beatin' the hell out of her-
                self, wantin' a new massacre where she finally
                makes it into the history books (all in the name
                of LENA)? that all the while i'd be simmerin'
                on the stove. gettin' burnt.

una parda, which is me

parda (feminine): a general term used in the spanish and portuguese colonies of the americas that referred to the mixed bloods whose ancestry could almost never be accurately described. for our purposes here, it is being used in reference to the multi-racial descendants of africans, natives, and europeans.

i am a perpetual pardon
i limp into the room &
you say: fox woman get out!
   smudge it & start again

i am naked & without clothing
i am the roasted house slave
i am the white man's leftovers
i am the white woman's hate
i am the high highfalutin rape
   smudge it & start again

i get seasick now that i'm older
the colonial in me is wearing away
but i still have that candle in the eye
called bloodlust
those kleptomaniac grabbers
it must have felt good wearing all that gold
i am a broke down ship   la niña
   smudge it & start again

nobody is a purebred anymore
i'm precocious mutt
i know all about the small living quarters for
tender-tribed-people like me
the people-with-too-many-ancestors-inside-of-us
we have now painted our living room
we chose the color of bloodied-up hide
we chose us

in the end i screech during childbirth
my husband takes off down the hall
like meaty antelope man
my skin is slick with sweat

i'm telling you it feels good to be this naked
forgive me you who are so fully clothed

ACT ! pose with fingers as though cigarette (puff puff)

once more unto the breach once more mama
has a bad habit of snickering every time i
say the word *theatre.* (thee-ate-her). jimmy
assigns me marriage to james. james goes
belly up trying to love me. i stare at him
deadly. jimmy believes this is quite sensual
of us (we never even touched). i am told to
perform the role of erykah badu head wrap
& the creation of incense. opening shot &
my hips are too small. the little black girl
inside me dies a little (o mama). the next
class they tell me i have tuberculosis, so
die already. i ask them politely to supply
the gun shot. next class they tell me i am
wild-haired virgin in the bronx who offers
myself up to first ding-a-ling to call me
savage in limbo. other schoolgirls are
such clementines, stelllaaaa, juliet with a
sky of flesh-cut stars. i am clov with post-
apocalyptic limp. clov who is black dust.
clov nursing his teeny tiny light. clov trying
to make an exit in jungle hat, but god bless
us, there's simply nowhere left. i scrape
baby hairs back. pencil in faux moustache
for devoted effect. twin tells me i'm not
busty enough to be an opera singer, a good
one at least (insert high note). i let james
fling me down on tables during rehearsal.
classmates really love this concussion of
mine. & this stye in my eye is a testament
of nostalgia (Dr. E believes such swelling is
a sign of severe loneliness). twin reminds
me that women with a light dusting of acne
have always been her favorite. director asks

if i have ever felt like a let-you-down. & sure jimmy, sure i have. haven't we all? on stage i'm trying to simulate some internal pink some veiny placenta truth. i'm left thinking of baby tigers at the national zoo. how pale & soft their tongues are. & do these stripes on display also cry? i've never seen it.

MAMI : a chest for healing

my head on your chest
when i fall asleep is when you fall asleep
i'm mumbling for the both of us

mami, tell me again how
big mother is a cast-iron pan with all that chitlin grease
how the cute boys down south
with their godfearin mothers suckin on hard candies
used to call you high yellow
they spotted the indian in you

tell me how big mother would sink a rag in hot turpentine oil
& pin it to your chest for healing
how her body was an hourglass with many tired years left
how she told you to be particular &
never let a boy play in your hair
how tender-headed you always were
   (i know you as my black hair sky)

remember how her daddy held you up to the light bulb
how he said you were born with a veil over your eyes
he saw you staring straight into the spirit world

there's this dream i have where
big mother's in the yard out back
teaching me about the wind
& i can't hear the tone of her voice
so i reach up for the zipper on her cotton housecoat
but she's really you
her face your face
her sturdy legs your somewhat skinnier legs

i do not feel big mother sitting at the foot of my bed with all our other ancestors
so forgive me as i go looking in all the earthly places
you've got that divine prerogative
i'm stuck at planet level
  (i know you as my worn-out saint)

tell me how she came to you in all your many visions afterwards
how big mother looked at you right before she passed
how her eyes crossed at the highest point on the ceiling
she saw something up there & finally caught it

PAPI : the swelling of scars in heat

papi, a rather severe face
a canine smile suggesting mischief
i was preordained to look more like you

i handed over prettier
twin to twin
because i have slightly different plans
i can't be red nails that glisten like cheap lava
just some offshoot between
jupiter optimus maximus & cigarettes

grandfather santiago was a woodcarver
papi, his very first figurine
& i know you felt all lacerations when
he revealed his final image of you
but here you are now
carving me up like old days

we're such generous caballeros
terrible at apologies
a vanity that speaks of
bejeweled magnificence from a past life
i'll call you crazy joe like they used to
if you call me blue

no way to explain in full
i am all the alcantara boys
not yet figuring themselves into men

papi, this poem as we know it
is not you but some other
beast entirely bowing its head for tenderness

see i cut off all my hair willingly
so that some day in the near future
when you ship me back to spain
to our dried-up vineyards
weeping as boys sometimes do
i might know how to use my hands

SANTIAGO SEIJAS FERNÁNDEZ PEREZ...ALCANTARA

abuelo, i think i am you. i think i am always combed back & slight north african features. i am also a fine-tuned alcoholic who cannot endure the gold-toothed hag that is america. i munch on paper just to get my words right. i believe myself to be a hellified woodcarver from time to time. to filet a friend over vino tinto y pulpo al ajillo, from chest to stomach & back again. we have a bad habit of noticing when a photo is hung just off center. of landing in jail for a night with our son. & because i am you i often walk into rooms & say something trivial like "it's got good bones."

i tell you this as you. because when we were dying from throat cancer we pulled out our own tube. we made sure there was an audience. & in that chair in the dining room blood flowed from the hole in our throat, stopping up our spirit. i was there slow clapping us to death. whistling in the back, saying "CARAJO, MANNNN. we really did it. it's a wonderful party we've thrown." never mind papi, tío, tomás the rabbit, abuela who died of an aneurism on the sidewalk shortly after.

abuelo, how did we leave papi in galicia counting seashells for so long? he was nothing but frantic limbs & no words to tell us how it hurt by the time he arrived in america. did we call him in those farewell months, just to hear his sticky little voice? how much english did we pick up off the floor, or, would you understand this poem if i handed it to you in the afterworld? i ask because i do not know all the details of our story the way i should. papi thinks you're some brandy-swigging, knife-wearing, well-meaning god. sometimes santiagos really are that grand.

i am fastened to papi now. born again as a woman so i must take care of him. (papi points emphatically to a photo of me when my face was much smaller & scrunched up, a rascally grin for the flash. "THAT'S WHO YOU ARE. THIS. YOU LET 'EM HAVE IT. I MEAN, YOU RIP 'EM TO SHREDS. THAT'S. YOU.") i think he's on to us. i think he knows.

YOUNG-HORSE-SO-YOUNG

i am mountain after
fire no hopi   zuni
just a pulsing little shard

i am young-
horse-so-young
i cannot stand
young-horse
i do not know
footprints

i threw up
blueberries
heaving into plum

cried while retching
my sainthood came
right on out
i felt large
self-excavation
of my indigenous
root onto lap onto
white embroidered dress
twin unzipped my back

i said i cannot stand
i said now a gap
a hole with no dirt

here in desert
i met you
tony

you asked what tribe
i answered young-horse-so-young you
released a yell

tony
we are both left hands
but you are am-bi-dex-trous

i offer you my left hands
so i can beat the
out-west-fragility out of me

you said focus i said focus
i said i am being torn wide open out here
i said i am being erased what to tell my parents

i throw myself
on all your sterling
silver & roll in
black beauty turquoise
plug my nostrils with gemstone
A WOLF IS A WILD DOG

come on &
teach
me

how to work my hands tony
how to make something
with my red like the wind
rendered new mexico
into hard rock
dirt dirt & dust
like you rendered this bangle
can i be your singular braid
can i nod off in your wide brim hat

this young-horse-so-young
is still tribeless
& my hooves have gone out again

i try not to attach myself to you
but i am your old polishing cloth
a useless thing

tony
wait for me
to come back now will you

i place all your jewels
in between my organs
i am a cut in this world
i've stood in the sun so long
my brains turned stew
soft spot too soft

great-great-grandfather it's you
come back as tony
saying your heart goes with me

great-great i believe
you are the oldest church
in native america

you believe the top
of my head is full of
too much light

great-great
i've got to ask you something now
while i've still got a hold of you now

will you please just skin me already
like one of them foxes the men

wear around their waists
will you whisper a prayer into my ears
lay me belly up & start in on the knifing
take my hide eat my body

great-great
i can be a heavy spirit
sitting at the foot of your bed i can be so great

these days all i can see is sorrel
these days i eat the desert &
i'm all dried up

I TOO WANT TO EAT THE WORLD

there are few men with an appetite for all
of the earth
its blueness
men who can then teach young girls
how to expand their jaws for such consumption
of blue
how to use their incisors to
cut such roundness
all of the black is blue

arthur mitchell died today !!
(these days one must say the thing twice)

MY MR. MITCHELL IS DEAD

see the whole world
they want to watch you
& clap only once you've performed   your corpse

BUT I WANT TO BE SHOT OUT OF A CANNON

i want to lunge at you
i want to grow five faces & tell you to kiss 'em
because truly my time on stage has been violent
i've given you the soles of my feet & my inner thighs
i gave to you   i gave of me to you   all of me to you

THE WORLD NEEDS A STRICT BLACK MAN

but the audience these days   the whole world   (lord have mercy)
is so white
there's no real winning here

you see   i know the ground   the six feet knocked nine feet under
with grief
                                    how to work with it
                    how to push off & become
              a whole solar system   myself

THE WORLD NEEDS A STRICT BLACK MAN

to hold its hand
              to hit its leg into the beat

                                        to put you on your leg to endure the turning
                              & in fifth position you only have one leg
                                        so if that leg fails you   well
                                            that leg better not fail you

              from mr. mitchell i inherited at a very young age
                    the knowledge of perfection
              from mr. mitchell i understood how to
                    make my body an arrow
              to be shot out into the audience at just the right time

                        WE NEED A STRICT BLACK MAN
                              TO COME OUT LIKE LIGHTNING
                        TO KILL US
                  WITH ELEGANCE WITH THE WAY
                  HE HOLDS HIS BACK & ARMS   he's nursing pluto

                        WE NEED A STRICT BLACK MAN
                  TO STARE STRAIGHT AT US & CONTINUE STARING
              STRAIGHT AT US
        UNTIL WE'VE DONE THE THING RIGHT   don't cry,
                              there's no point to all that

i am a very small black woman
so small in fact
my color has faded
causing me to be a very shy child
but when that man held my hand
i hurled myself onstage
like a devil baby
i stared straight out with my arms so wide
& i died i died   i died

I'M A BLACK BLACK BLACK BLACK BLACK BLACK TAN WOMAN

i can't talk about my black because it ain't their black
so i just ain't black. i drag up mama for proof.

everybody considers mama as not my mama,
airport officials hastily conclude

"she is not part of the family."
spot. GORGEOUS. BLACK. SPOT.

on all our hands. my mama
has done it all.

i listen to her recordings &
sob when she croons to me

from her very black gut.
i feel her like life

threadbare before me.
mama was lady macbeth once.

i concentrate
on this while hypnotizing

8:40 AM Scene Lab classmates
with my monologue.

afterwards teacher prostrates
at my feet.

i say, "you better thank my mama."
my mama is clear outta this world.

& i'm her daughter so i'm her kind
of black.

LOOKING IN THE MIRROR WHILE TRYING ON LEOTARDS

                    someone once asked me if dance is sensual
as a dancer   "no"
    their response back : not necessarily , but   maybe ?
                & again i said "no ,   not ever"

my tummy is not a 6-pack like twin's
       always   one twin has more womanly hips
   the costumes are semi-see-through-
     nipples peak out from under   i'm a
                  youngladyyoungladyyoung
      articles on how to ask your dancers
    to dance naked & why
            naked matters   does it matter ???
because the general public are freaks
they love the body as a descaled fish
   the body as a fish with a cavity where its guts should be
   the body as a function

         mark the exercise with music   chicken arms !!
    lift   hold the leg in midair for e i g h t h o u r s
adagio is a killer
    i walk out the room   pretend to drink at the water fountain
someone looks in the mirror
   at me sweating
     the pianist plays too fast   we all crush on the pianist ,
    wish he'd look at us more   girls are ridiculous like that

i was staring at the back of the person in front of me at barre
    she has scoliosis i thought
     turn to the other side   i thought it was cute   her bacne
boys also have stretch marks
         boys also wear thongs

my teacher presses her hand through the back of my ribcage &
pushes me forward   over my hips
     i can barely move my legs   she says GOOD GIRL
               i'm such a young lady   i can still dance
     it will only cost $$$159.00 for my father to buy & install a barre
in our family home
                    my muscles twitch in sleep due to overuse

     undressing behind pianos
   costume designer shows up & we're all shaved
                         he fits me into barely anything at all
          he looks away as i shimmy in

               & i say "don't be silly
     carter, it's me
       you've seen me before
          just a young lady   just a body"
                         i do not want flat-footed-children

i used to force twin to take polaroids of my
          adolescent feet en pointe
                    my teachers say STOP . SICKLING . YOUR FEET .
     but it's hard
   it's hard when
                    you're bowlegged
   when the lights on stage make you sheen earlier
                    when your partner grips both your armpits

     the hold is necessary so you don't crack your skull again
     so you don't go backstage &
     hold your head in the only stall available
     the pink of your brain a throb
     the other dancers do not mention the drop
     no one wants to talk about the drop
     you peel off the wet leotard
     the same one you'll wear tomorrow night
     you spray vodka on it so the sweat doesn't smell

you go out into the lobby
where some old lady starts talking at you
& the young lady inside your young lady is eating a writhing fish
its scales are a nascent blue & they're shimmering
you blink back at the woman
with three sets of eyes
you turn off the lights
you hear the ambulance speeding
you think you walk out

estocada

when i was six
i watched a bull
get pierced to death

by a slicked back
man in
pulled up tights

    (what i would have done to wear that choked up jacket)

it is exhausting
a portly stone arena
of spaniards

rasping with impeccably starched
handkerchiefs to kill
this black thing

    (i'm wanting to hold firm onto your trembling toro bravo weight)

mami & papi
pulled me up before
sword through neck

blood glistened on
hair hips thrusted
flat slippers for lunging

    (marry me or kill me but no more cape)

i hooked my neck & cried

        to kill such a thing
        to kill such a thing that is already dead
        take my tail & stew it

FIERCER STILL, FIERCER YET

showing off nana's red silk lingerie
i am splayed out on the couch
legs all o p e n &
i am not a female poet
i am of the male variety
o the slack i'm cut
when i'm this all-knowing muscle
how unrestricted it is within me
for i too have wrestled a man to the
floor i have punched my own brother
i have licked his blood from the wall later that night
it's brutal
the way i sleep
with my fists wound so tightly up
like my father i am my father & also his father
i am most likely therefore all the fathers
in the yearbook i was named "most likely to kill someone with my eyes"
twin was "most likely to start world war iii"
& this is just the reality we live in
i am my father at age 25
i am my father yelling in the streets
walking all bowlegged
i am here on this couch
with my limbs so far apart
thinking of all the ways i've been known to–
WATCH ME WRITE IN ALL CAPS SUCKA
see that's not what i wanted at all
LISTEN TO ME
i have the capacity within my bones
i just have to reach into my blood & pull it out
the damn thing gets stuck sometimes
in the ovaries
it gets stuck
in the ovaries in the uterus

as they say my machismo gets stuck
in this slightly tilted uterus of mine
the doctoress reached so far up
i thought she touched rib
i thought she whispered *adam*
& i whimpered because
it wounded me this being-a-woman business
my skin suit stretched from the inside
with two fingers i am not a female poet
the ferocity of my body as the female body as the male body i am the white male body
the things i take for granted
for i am zeus
a totally erotic cult figure
with too many heinous children
it's brutal
the way i sleep
with my fists wound so tightly up
the permanent wrinkles in my sheets

//   \\

desert room #1 (ten thousand waves spa)

we drove higher up. three feet away from night sky & stripped to our skins.
in the women's communal tub everyone was bared.
shea did leg exercises underwater.
i laid out rib on wooden floor. stuck leaves to my chest.
twin plunged into cold water & tested how long she could stay in
until her nerves gave out. we all ended staring up.
the sky is a perineal laceration out west.
in the grand bath there were men & a waterfall.
i moved my feet back & forth in the warm water.
i was still a watercolor from the dislodged blueberries of morning.
it was hard not to feel tender when i was constantly being tenderized.
it was hard not to call all the bodies jiggling around in their skins *dear*.
we were all a litter beginning to grow light. our eyes a haze.
bones not fully baked.
before my shower i saw a man writing messages onto little foam cups.
i asked him if he was a poet.
he said we're all sand in the end.
the decomposition of your face will be a sad thing.
i told him i'm getting cremated.
he stopped his scribble to glance up at me.
he pointed at my navel & said very cute cut.
he pointed at my head & said ahhh the globe.

desert room #2 (santo domingo pueblo)

THIS IS THE SIGN FOR THE CORN
DANCE. THIS IS THE SIGN FOR
OUTSIDE FOLK. IT SAYS YOU
CANNOT DO ANY OF THE THINGS,
STRANGER. I AGREE. I DO NOT DO
ANY OF THE THINGS. NO CAMERA.
NO NOTE. THIS IS NOT A NOTE,
STRANGER. I CANNOT SPEAK
ABOUT THE WOMEN WITH HAIR
LIKE BLANKETS. THE SMOOTH
STOMPING OF FEET TO DESERT
FLOOR. THE MEN RINGING WITH
SOMETHING THAT SOUNDS LIKE
THE VOICE AFTER THE VOICE
HAS UP AND LEFT. THE SMOOTH
STOMPING OF FEET TO DESERT
FLOOR. HERE, I AM NOT RIGHT.
THIS SNOW CONE IS DELICIOUS.
MY MOUTH IS BLUE. I STARE AT
THE PLAZA WITH THE BODIES. I
BUY THE VERY SOFT SILVER OF
THE BODIES, CALL IT A BADGER
OUTSIDE OVEN RED MESA CARVED
INTO BRACELET. I ASK ABOUT THE

FAT PICKLES SWIMMING IN KOOL-AID. THE HOUSES WITH TOO MANY PEOPLE SITTING ON FLAT ROOF TOPS. I WANT TO YELL DO NOT FALL. YOU ARE FALLING. I FELL ONCE. LISTEN TO MY TRIBAL RULES AND REGULATIONS:

1. WHEN THE NATIVES ASK YOU TO HEAD INSIDE THE THREE-WALLED HUT, SLURP ALL THE BROWN STEWS. DO NOT ASK FOR VEGETARIAN OPTIONS.

2. WHEN THE BABYGIRL IN THE PLAZA WALKS STRAIGHT UP TO YOU, SHE WILL GRAB YOUR HEAD AND CALL IT THE SUN. SHE WILL TELL YOU TO BE CAREFUL, OR ELSE YOU WILL BURN YOURSELF STRAIGHT TO THE GROUND.

3. YOU ARE UNA PARDA AGAIN. PART OF A TRIBE SET ON FIRE. ANOTHER TRIBE OF GOD. ANOTHER TRIBE THAT IS BARED. CUIDADO. TEN CUIDADO.

4. ALLOW THE BABYGIRL TO PLACE SOME STICKY WORDS ON YOU. YOU NEED A MOTHER OUT HERE, OFF INTERSTATE 25.

5. THANK HER. KISS BOTH HER LITTLE PALMS. THE SMOOTH STOMPING OF FEET TO DESERT FLOOR.

6. FALL BACK DOWN INTO THE DUST. IT IS AUGUST AND YOU MIGHT JUST BE A SIGN STUCK OUTSIDE. YOU MIGHT JUST BE FRIED FISH.

desert room #3 (el rey court)

the geriatric couple in the pool
  looks at us like we won't get in

        twin & shea slink into the shallow end
      black & red hair fanning out behind them
      a couple of waxy lily pads

  my much-loved night swims
    the underwater lights hitting your body
  a volvo xc90 coming straight for you

          i sit on the white & tangerine pool chair

      the old couple drips away &
      i hear my two lily pads laughing again
        the way women laugh that is really a bark

  i would like to know where to place myself
upright in the parking lot   bent in the hotel restaurant seat   flat out across the bed
    in the native life i have not lived

          in my head the italian director is preaching to me & twin
        he says "go back to your elders & ask them about the plants."
          i want to say:
          "WHAT PLANTS?
            WHERE ARE MY ELDERS?
        FIND THEM. BRING ME BACK MY INFORMATION."

on the floor of the pool
    cobalt waves are painted
  even water isn't enough
      the deeper dagger of my multidimensional existence

just this morning i got my aura photographed &
from the root of me i burnt straight through the frame
the lady said "jesus, you're the sun."
i said "i know. it hurts.
who wants to be so isolated?
where are my planets? you all promised me at least eight very good planets."
the lady ran out the store
her head one gold flame

i said "i'm sorry.

when i'm hurting the flames come like that.
it's not my fault. i'm still learning."

i fall straight down into the chlorination
& find myself floating up

i can't hear the barking anymore
just water going straight in the ear holes
a ringing that is lily pad howling

i look at those puffy little stars
become raceless
don't need all those planets anymore
maybe just a moon

i move my arms back & forth
my two lily pads blooming in the distance
to cool down for just a bit

fox woman saunters back

i am loose-limbed   woman
sudden on my black-tipped toes   fine ears and underfur
wind between trees

i've been stuck in this viridescent landscape
a hazy film where i strike along the base of forest
where my cunning becomes feminine

i am praying for all the bodies
i am asking for light
i am asking to get out of this verdant dreamscape

i did not mean to outrun your gun
with your eyes fixed on my snout
you wanted flattened skull and underfur

i did not mean to scream
the way a woman does in distress
i did not mean to ravage your inner flesh

i am praying for all the bodies
i am asking for light
i will not wound you again

i am too many
    trees between wind
 long jagged teeth
  someone's reddish brown love

||| ||

we.are.old.everything.is.old.

(scene one: all these herringbone floors)

twin, we've been here before. barrel vault ceilings. rich suits standing uptight. our scene is set. we just have to enter.

tonight you say we're well-to-do apes. full knuckular braggadocious & head up for holler. i grab a fistful of lady hair before you mouth *no, not that.*

i'm remembering now how hot it becomes up against all our fur. the women are too dainty, so i try to break them in more ways. again you tell me, *we're not here for that. the suits are meant to watch us. no touching. we are going to perform.*

we move on to our luchador mask bit. tonight i handle all the high-flying maneuvers. but, because i skipped our rehearsals, i don't know what lock to put you in for a win. you keep scrambling out from underneath me. i didn't properly tie my mask. the vinyl doesn't grip the front of my face quite like yours. i cannot see through the eye slits anymore. this makes us laugh.

in the next act i am pregnant. the belly suits me just fine. you run around the accumulation of suits with me on your back. we are dashing to the birth of jupiter's 81st moon & everyone is in the way. my clear white milk hits the herringbone floor. some of the suits want to wipe this up, but they don't. they hold their pocket squares firmly.

next we settle into our haunches & take turns tapping each other on the third eye until it turns into quite a whacking, as if to say: WAKE THE HELL UP, TWIN. THIS LIFE. IT'S TIME.

i go around declaring: I AM NO LONGER AS PRECIOUS AS I REMEMBER MYSELF BEING. & then you & i call each other precious for the rest of the night. WHY YES, PRECIOUS IS DOING JUST FINE.
OH, MMM, PRECIOUS WILL BE ELATED TO HEAR YOU LIKED THE THIRD EYE BIT.
NO, PRECIOUS DOES NOT REGRET PULLING YOUR HAIR OUT. IT WAS GOOD GOOD ART.

by the end i recognize your scribble on the herringbone floor: a deconstruction of the modern-day love novel starring two twin beasts. & the audience is sad for us because our love is written & therefore dead.

after the show is over, after our fur is slick with sweat, the suits clap their manicured hands. we bow our skulls softly. we ape out the same way we entered. knuckular. overused. we tell the clapping suits, ALL GOOD THINGS GROW MUCHACHITOS. ALL GOOD THINGS GROW.

(scene two: changing room chat)

in our changing room we stare at the very large mirrors & all that's left is our breathing. you give a gold-toothed laugh & say *remember, we are gods.* i chuckle too. *poor suits, they had no idea.*

in a second we recall that we.are.old.everything.is.old.

the suit who invited us here tonight knocks on our door & enters. i pat his left cheek, you his right & the three of us smile in this huddle. twin, i catch a glimpse of you in the mirror & can't help but think what a cult leader you would make. charming with your broad shoulders & modest touch.

suit tells us we must come back for another show. we slink into the couch & say politely, *no, we don't feel like it.* suit grows older in his dissatisfaction. you tell him to take a seat. i grab his left hand in mine & say, *we've thought about it & we don't know what good it is anymore. showing suits our wounds & asking them for a good licking to help seal it up. we saw our own films & we don't understand the pretense ourselves. we are not so sure we are people anymore, so, what use are we to suits?*

for our next & final piece we want you to construct for us the world's largest cage. let the cage be a mansion actually. & call us both lena. for a month, let the suits enter this house at their leisure. let the suits watch us rearrange our house slippers, this ritual of our oncoming apogee, watch us fully realize what a dream we all are. when the month is up, you must let us out of the cage & we will go on, turn over into two twin mounds of earth. dear suit, never forget, the earth is a body, a very large body, your mother in fact, & she's waiting.

one day, suit, stop crying, please. here, give me your right hand, place it on the top of my skull. one day, dear suit, you will go to some far edge of your universe & see us two mounds. you will speak to us & in our silence you will understand our speech entirely. suit, you are not like the other suits. you are something purer. come visit us as mountains, once the transformation is complete, & you will understand a gold-toothed smile amongst the three of us. suit, you look very handsome tonight. you may remove your right hand from my skull & i will let go of your left hand. lena will commence holding both your hands for eight more minutes. then you can go out & tell the suits what it is you think you know.

& twin, true to my words you hold on to him & he weeps like our son, so we tussle him around like all good beasts do, to lighten his furrow. we say *go now, suit. we love you. we do.*

(scene three: the two lena's walk)

we wash the beasts off our bodies & leave the same way we came: cigarette smoke trailing from my right hand, though there is no cigarette to be seen. twin, you with all your virgin mary necklaces. such protection, yes, you would make a wonderful cult leader indeed. we walk away from suit knowing he will never make it to us as the lena mounds. & i almost start weeping for him until you stare at me & say, *no, not that*. & i remember, we are gods. you are the spiral arms of the milky way galaxy & i am red clay. *all the same in the end*, you mutter.

we set to walking slowly & you grab my hand in your twin hand, & when i say i'm unsure about all this cage & mound business, because what if my own end makes me miserable, you just stare at me for eight whole minutes. you take out your camera & we make one last film of it. you tell me i should imagine i am in the canyons again & suddenly the crying comes harder. it's nightfall here & i want to reclaim my clayness. like any true director you never quit rolling. you zoom into my eyes & say, *we are like babes*. i agree. i understand human exhaustion, the livelihood of something other than apes.

& then i come to it: *mounds are not so bad*. you say, *one day, lena, we will all return back from whence we came & then, there we are again. same old same old. not much changes at home, but we always come back to it so crushed, some of us enlarged. god bless us. the ones with too much light in their skulls will pray to us because they understand this much. & the suits, the poor suits, they will continue to look for us as we are now, waiting & wanting us to squeeze ourselves out for their pleasure. & when they stumble upon us as mounds, well, my sweet sweet lena, they won't even know we're there.*

C o N T I n e n T A L

max, you were right
about the gum around the bones   reincarnation
& other max, you were also right
about a rock star being
nothing more than an egomaniac hiding from the tragedy of their own existence

the three of us (max & max & india)
,i'd like to think,
often wonder about the big A
(authenticity)

remember *& swan song*??? (the dance piece)
how the audience examined us uncertainly
& then wept
were we being straight out there???

dear reader(s), i am assuming you are lost now
you do not believe in such tiny sparks of divinity
& yet, a couple of you must (not all third eyes can be easily ulcerated)

in a past life i was kublai khan, a whole tectonic plate
i cannot make this up
this is the big A

& the mere thought of yet another life kills me, i mean it, it obliterates me
i want no more lewis & clark expedition

i want to crawl back in utero
into the pink gummy gummy between mama's legs
(goodbye max & max)

twin

    you & i are

    rama & lakshmana

follow me into this thick thick forest

        let us see what we can make of it

    like the tiniest of wolves

what to do when all your good fur starts receding
(mother & father are good things)

have you ever heard
a beluga hum so lowly
for their indistinguishable

my grandfather as elegance
my father crosses-his-legs
he sits
how lovely the men can be sometimes

mother is well-made
mother appears sandalwood
mother overthrows father

when i dream-die i do not want
hidden in breast are precisely
two very good secrets
(in twenty nine years
they will mostly be revealed)

twin listens to floorboards twice daily
she talks to me about they talk to her
when the sun dies   amurrrica

what to do when your stockings lead to more sensuality than you're worth
when all your legs go missing
when your thumbs turn celeste
(imagine you are dreaming of two largely bodies   )

the cellos are calling me back three lives over
father's bass   mother's diaphragm

i am   going to pick up   the   phone   s l o w l y   now

when i was three i could hear my father, i could let down hair, the good fur, mother
watched from a slit in the stairs, mother was
a chair, mother was a slit in the stairs, &
truthfully, dear god, i could not stop dancing

until just now

for my future babies

the heartbeats in the room
have mostly disappeared but
this patch of forest is mine to give you

to my sons
it's been whole lemons & strawberries

having such little bodies
to dedicate my time to
all our baths

pink calamine like dalmatian spots
your growing into ankles

i hope you recall your childhood
as watercolors out back
as long hair being combed through

to my daughter
you are cool light
before the sun dies

(o how i revere you!)

how you take your earthen feet
crawl your way up my bare legs
to my stomach to my chest

when we are face to face
you rub my head with honeyed hands
give me a quick kiss before climbing bigger trees

darlings, would you believe me if i told you
that i've stretched my arms
so long
to hold you throughout

that i was born pregnant
with the very vision of
you

BELUGA

i remember when your bones outgrew your   skin
mama rubbing fermented   banana leaf
like a prayer all over you

who goes first this time?

hermanita
siempre hemos sido ballenas   beluga

pero   qué más sucede después?

very   blue   water
&   the   echo   of   our   great twin   mouths

IN MY DREAMS THEY CALL ME TENOCHTITLÁN

I AM MUD
I AM SLUGGING my body back home
        whole volcanoes lose their juice

                     & twin   the most terrible thing happens
        when the body starts shaking the trauma
     never stops
   & when you're a glutton for the failing sun
rigor mortis sets
       teeth baring   for dinner you expected meat   big boar

at the mouth of a well we found jade   in the tooth   human jaguars & paw
     they said   hernán cortés
       & true to all good history
  twin   ,   my sweet
     pedro de alvarado ,
       we set our hands right
     played antagonist
                    lunged first

               i was reaching for mother but
        she passed into mesoamerican sand
          father: her baroque architecture

     horror becomes my half-breed face (so histrionic so
                      swollen)

once our hands set to carving we lost a whole finger

         twin   the seas have gifted me such sly limp
      i shall throw off my shirt & shuffle towards you
    you with such long hair lace ruff holding up neck

   this year jungle is all we have left
    inner edge of pyramid

where soul aligns with limestone
                              call us profoundly brutus

how to tell the natives we are them   we are holy   &   rock
if you are reading my letter from the coast   why the preemptive slaughter
        dear pedro ,   there's no graceful way to end this

                                      YOU MUST carve the god out of me
                                                    now

            o the hollows of the earth for living   a bowl for the body

i am dusky narcissus   i stared too deep
                disassociated from the self
        am nothing but echo
                    this face completely went awry
        in 1521
                        mother witnessed

                                    i fell off the tree in sleep
                                        no hypnic jerk to save
                                                my civilization declined
        & rapidly at that   i must have died

        the paling because we cannot   polysynthesize   agglutinate
        i want their very bitter chocolate
            comet mother teach me the scorpion stars   the eschatology
of the four worlds
                        rubber balls & hips saying "death is for the winners"

SPLIT ME WIDE OPEN & SUCK MY SEEDS RIGHT OUT
                        WEAR MY RAWHIDE PELT AS THE GOD SKIN

the body so well preserved

as if the body mattered

                                   i wanted to see them RUNNNNN

        don't let the arrow pass
    through gut

horror becomes my half-breed face (so histrionic so
                                      swollen)

                                   as if my body mattered at all

all the matriarchs in spain are dead

mami & papi tell us to take off our swimsuit tops
to stop being so american
twin & i hug our chests

our apartment in barcelona is full of shrimp & donuts & coltrane
roberto at summer camp sits next to twin on the bus
he talks small english

he breaks my headband
because he loves my twin he buys me five new headbands
i get a black eye playing pool

                                                tía nona   tía nona
                                                          tía nona

at the waterpark
us & the boys are tiny torsos   sticks for legs   i run fast but twin is faster
we eat ice cream   wear goggles   our hair in double buns

franchie is a real caballero   a lover boy   twin's future husband
carlos is our cousin   he slaps twin in the face when she wins the soccer game
our fathers curse each other out for the next half hour

tía dochi

after all the matriarchs in our family died i thought
all of spain was supposed to be my throne
twin & i have stolen all the crucifix necklaces preparing
for my eventual coronation
i know who is the first to be beheaded
twin has stitched endless amounts of velvet to my back
we've spent hours considering los campesinos
i rehearse my two phrases for the court
PUTA MADRE & NO. NO. NO.
twin has searched all of spain for my future king
she says her stick legs hurt
he still does not exist
& i respond PUTA MADRE. NO. NO. NO.

tía fina   abuelita   tía fina

emma is the goat who lives on top of rafa's house
palomita is the mutt who keeps giving me fleas
i will not stop petting them

abuelita

tía nona
tía dochi
tía fina
abuelita

you all are tough bread left out overnight
a side of strawberry jam
you pull my teeth out

when i tear away at the dough of you
i love your catholic ways & frizzy hairs
i love your hands washing my clothes
your fingerprints all over me

the bath water is too cold in early morning
twin & i huddle together shivering
papi says *get in & get out that's the trick*

mami says *go out with the boys & make sure you dress warm*
franchie walks us across town
at the beach old men splash water onto mami's ankles
papi throws me into the deep end of the pool so i can learn to swim

            abuelita   abuelita   abuelita
               nuestra abuela   abuelita

                              abuelita

I'M STILL ALIVE

movimiento núm. uno

this is not an accident
the outro to our movie
(wind thru tha hair, yes)
mama venus womb of sticks & red gooey
LIFT UR HUSKY LEG
we're all dying together
LIFT BOTH UR HUSKY LEGS
(wind thru tha hair, yes)
u are no longer beautiful
until u stomp back down
start the wrasslin with who?
father uranus? ur stick men babies?
somehow i have failed u
hermetic hunnies AGITATE
(wind thru tha hair, yes)
because who are u
writing for these days?
this elevator is broken
o we have no moons no moons no moons
praise be

movimiento núm. dos

so in this shot it's
(i am forever slowing myself down to last longer)
real human hands & femur
MOSTLY BONEY THEN THERE'S MEATY
also a little dirty
like that smile, boys?
i've got all my adult t-e-e-e-t-h
in case u noticed

my fantasy of hippos
o i wanted
i wanted
their four-toed hooves
sunburnt skin
salamander digits touch me please
i'm not sure what will come
but i promise it's good

movimiento núm. tres

bandit women
punch.   punch. punch.
o tha cowboys always let us down
cardboard boys behind
toothpick & gunslinger
how they crush tha animal
masks on desert floor
after long days of thick-necked mountain
my bandits
this is dead heat
punch.   punch. punch.

movimiento núm. cuatro

it's just a gesture
it's just a hand gesture
i didn't write it
it just exists

movimiento núm. cinco

i must
to say i

(no)
to say me
o me o me o me
o
to say push me down this cliff
to say ACT !
to say ACT ! again
otherwise this is never more
to say i did not separate myself from this
to say it's taken me a looooong   time   to   drown
to get here
& dear seasick sailors
that's O.K.
to ask DO U FEEL ME? HOW DO U? DO U?
to handle the no no n o noooo no no
to say WOW
really
to say o u
carve into ur freedom
o tha skin suit falls right off
o a waste of a good body (a good boy)
i love it
o bye friends
to say i want to make cosmic affection
with u
to say
o hi baby pluto
my exile my boy
to say from outer space
of glitter & darkness
WOW THIS IS DARKNESS
BUT O WOW THIS IS GLITTER TOO
LOOK AT ALL THIS TIIIIIIIMMME MAMA!!!
(i'm the second brightest object in the sky)
to say i still feel tha dinos walking
to say i saw i saw
to go

to say i did not make this by mistake
but my nana o my nana
& her brandied duck
she is sundown scorpio
fading & her words come out
defeated O NANA
i'll fall out this window again
i'll fall out just to make u
i'll fall out just to make u very much
alive again
& yes it's saturn again
i still hate u saturn
it's very much too late for anything else
this is my guts on tha operation table
orangutan, right twin???
orange or-an-gu-tang & it hurts
o it hurts it hurts it hurts!!
but i must go/will/am
yes munching whole pomegranate
(i wanted as many seeds!)
i run
she run
they all runs
o man o   man   ooooo man
my seeds
they're a spillin'
i'ma gammy on all ma gammies
i go

fox woman strikes back

it is true
                        my power lies   at dusk   &   dawn
            between times
        when spirit   &   world intersect
                                    when bright &   shade bend their backs

                                    it is true
                                i live at border
                                                edge of
                            forest
                                            watching   the humans

        the men have gone hunting
                they have mistaken me for prey   for wife
        they have aimed their fine arrows in my direction   sharp flint teeth they've
                                                                    become
                thought me fox only
                                shot
                                    found a dead bush
not this woman
                                    //   \\

                        i am building   shaping   anew \\   world
                    creating the beginning again
                                    but first death
                                        first the old must go out

            //

                    the men have gone hunting
    they have aimed their weapons   all lined up
        i have beguiled them
        leaping in front of their man-made temper
        chasing my own tail   (turned it into flame to offer them fire   the fools)

77

                    rolling   frisking   curtsying
                        i drew closer   closer
                            i laughed with pointed muzzle
                            bounding   &   twisting
                                    i barked
                        i waited
                        tiptoed   like   s w e e p i n g
                    i created a circle
                    waited
                never falling out of breath
            waited

until they thought i was just the performer
some silly woman
the vixen   (with my ugly little fangs   \   the ravaged flesh called inner cheek   )

i waited
until i didn't

//

                        unless the men can understand
                        the divinity of femininity
                        inherent in themselves and others

                        they will suffer
                        the /fractured\   pregnancy
                        the never giving birth
            still   the carrying of all that weight

their blood   :a specific juice

                            //

i heard your spirit
during la noche oscura
& i came to wrap you in my infinite tail
to give you warmth
your spirit settled down just then
sank back into your body
you'll want to know how to speak with me
you'll want to remember
i did not leave you scorched like the others

               //   \\

            to contract   deep pelvic muscles   spine grow i n g l o n g
                   this   the
           vertical ribs   this the   sweat
           i slink on   woman
always   the   subtle   mother

//

just as you've been watching me
i've been watching you

& waiting
always waiting

\\

        a mother
        gives birth
        standing upright
        & when baby drops out
        in its bubblegum pouch
        mother starts off the
        booting with back leg
        bubblegum pouch glides
        &

mother keeps looking back
                between kicks
in a pool of her own bloodslip

this looks like agony
            beautiful (originating from brute, the bastard)
it bursts   opens its small small mouth for panting

mother keeps on pushing
baby to stand
baby starts peg-legged walking
mother is never done

intimacy is just violence
with a new name
the semi-suicidal performance of worldly love

if you don't name it
it doesn't exist
            you can't perform it
            so i don't say WORLDLY LOVE
                                i don't say it
for what is a fox woman to love exactly?
            what in this material world do i really love?   the notion of warmth?
    & is that love, that deep fire we tend to religiously in our stomachs?
how shall that love deliver us past the precipice of death?
                how do you take it with you if you only worship the form?
    what shall i think i know well enough to call its name?
                                academia :   another sort of privileged death
        why shall i macerate the words to create a false start
                                                in such cheap fashion ?

        //
            i shall make a world in silence
        & the new ones shall not speak
                    they shall not say   \\
            & everything will remain one mammoth   unspoken prayer

      & they will know
   in their silence they will know me
        for who i am

          //

my soft   wet   pulpy masses   (how to birth the formless into form and why?)
the placenta never came   (so love can take more forms, more
                     containers to fill, so many plastic containers)
so i kept on pushing   lightning
mother is never done. mother is never done. mother is never done. i am telling you.

//

i have given birth to myself
held myself close underneath the covers of indigo sky
& that too is shakti
that too will kill you   \\

nana was the first fox i knew
before i knew myself as fox
nana was a woman set on fire
a mighty sequoia tree
she was always growing up & up & up & up & up & up   & out
her arms were   extended
     a good god

       when it rains outside i rain too

you have to understand
this is all i know :   the body is not big
               before it dies   no   it's not
     but nana was still tall   still sequoia   still growing in spirit
      & she remains large in my mind   she fills me up   she remains
    this is all i've ever known   about being a woman
      if you are not careful   it can disembowel you
    if you are not careful   you can pay too much attention to one form

& then you die without that sequoia making itself known
taking real root within you   you will die having never really known

    //

        here is another unleashing

                        //

i never wanted the hunt   (would not have created it myself   have not   )
to kill or be killed
i never wanted
to keep one shape
one voice
one truth
death   (yet another unleashing   )
   i am   forever woman   yes   a whole   sequoia   (i love you   nana   lena
still cannot give you up   )
many faces
        the matrix of the unborn
& just when you think you understand me
just when you think you've seen me in plain sight
just when you think i am standing where i am no longer standing
        i will arrive home as your mother
      pregnant yet again with the thought of you as a peaceful man

the heart beats so large i cannot sleep

this is my magnum opus (!!!): that i have loved you and you never came. that i still love you cold, with no potential for warmth.

somewhere there is a head of dampened soil, no waxing petals, no length of stamen or stem. no thing to grow. is that what you passed along, big mother? the knowledge of self—excuse me death. how to die and when and why. not everyone can drop off like that. fall off the cliff with such ease. see, the way we do it, the spirit ain't going or gone. the way y'all taught me, i'll soon drop off this dangling sediment (what a life!) and certainly that is peace, that i have loved you and you never came. how many times did you die in a workweek? that i still love you cold, with no potential for warmth. big mother, how much of yourself did you give away to silence? did that not also feel dead? did you really feel living? at least once? i have been moving but motion is not living. this is my magnum opus (!!!), that around the next river bend all of you are waiting like a leash of foxes to welcome me to the sweltering den. that is a lie. this is my magnum opus (!!!): that i am reheated. overheated. molten. and it feels so good. yet another lie, a performance, if you will. my magnum opus: i ought to leave you all alone. out of respect. i ought to stop saying your names like this, calling on you with such dying heat. do you want me to stop, big mother? rest, big daddy? stop. please. lay down beside me here, wherever here is. just this once. and i won't tell no one. i won't say a word about how good it felt resting up against your flush fur. please lay down beside me on this bed of grass, on my head of grass (some things can grow, i suppose, if you give them enough time). my grass pulled to the side, parted for your leisure, for your unworldly weight. i can bear it. i can bear it. i can bear it. i can bear it. i can bear it. i can bear your unworldly weight. stop and please come, all of you. please do not pass me by. please sleep while i am sleeping. please make sure to watch over me, to conserve my dying efforts, to help me contend with living. this is my magnum opus: that

i am always a far ways away from my people. i am always too far. ain't it? i climbed up to the mountain top and verily dear lord i created fire. they weren't there. verily dear lord the fire grew as a signal to come, to arrive, to stop passing me by just this once. they still aren't here. i am always exerting always exerting always attempting life. what's left? what now that i am gutted through and through? this inflamed magnum opus. that i have loved you cold, with no real potential for warmth.

mama wonders how long big mother would have lived if mama had stayed in south carolina. but she couldn't. she couldn't live staying like that. for that type of living was verily a death, and big mother knew it, so she went ahead and willed her passing. what's been passed down to you? i know tired. i know tired too well. there is a way in which mama always stayed beside big mother, whispering in her ear, rubbing her head like she did mine as a child when i could not go to sleep. eventually mama had to go to sleep. eventually i would play my bed frame like a drum to fall asleep. i would create a rhythm with my left hand for calling my ancestors to help me fall asleep. my rhythm was not a beautiful song, for it was the soundings of this child. eventually sleep came, but i cannot say it was good, i cannot say i am well-rested. there is a way in which mama does not tell me everything. where mama also goes silent. and i want to know what goes on there, in that silence. i want to know silence without harm. there is a way in which mama beams at big mother and tells her she'll take her out of that place, she'll take her anywhere she wants to go. days before she passes. before she goes. there's a way in which i'm still telling mama that: pick a place, any place at all, just spin the globe goddamnit. how far can i take you and where and when? there's a way in which big mother came back from her travels, looking like herself through me to tell mama she'll take her any place she wants to go. right now. just say a place. right now. just pick a place right now. and i'll take you there right now. anywhere but here right now. i promise.

«« ««

afterwor(l)d

with the (w)ringing of self   something kin to silence

he(a)r(t) knowledge : i have died by other names

the ritual of our collective rebirth ,   still   not the reality

we start for the last time   there is solace in that

we start by laying down the self proper   then we let it go   that
heaviness

no longer owning any thoughts   post-mind collaboration

new dimensions revealed

and my pups lay by the river   as goodness   catching sun on too soft fur

they leave their bodies behind

this is still not death

they are laying down the self proper   just let it go

leaving behind the molecular

please do not think   this is forgetting   this is the very
definition of

remembering one's self

this type of living   feels like   water   heavy rushes of water
consistent blue   with no body-frame to catch it   still   the overflow

of liquid falls   hits large rocks   (i know   the feeling   )

what remained of them was   dancing   undomesticated dancing   rapture
extended up & up & up & up & up & up   & out

                    do you know what i know ?   or more ?   or less ?

imagine what it is for the skyline to be not a line but a great depth of color to fall
into or away from   viscous paint to go swimming in   you are strong enough
to make it out   i promise   but the color may stain you   (who are you
anyway?)

                    imagine your self as tidal wave

you may be thinking (stop thinking) an eruption is bound to occur somewhere
near
  no more
of that

        the volcano never formed

    nothing here is ever hot enough to melt   or even singe

that is love , no?   that
                                        feeling

                    my pups belong to the existence of a greater Mother (dirt dirt)

my pups   who know the truth behind their birth   are kind to offer me
    motherness

the truth   this is still the same wor(l)d you grew up in   just a narrow egress

the truth   i did not run away from your wor(l)d   i ran in   i ran in   i ran
inside my self   and   she   was hardened   with bloodied-up hide

        i . am . not . tethered . to . this . wor(l)d .
                                        I HAVE TO SAY THAT

CLEARLY   AT LEAST ONCE

                        i . am . not . tethered .

                                                i .

(((inside my self   still   the imprints of fetal pups   the space
i cannot help but keep   i cannot help but   feel   their
pre-birth weight   the faint pull of their   small-boned gravities   )   )   )

                                the very image of the AM

let me grow this spirit mouth (alas   )

thr is no one   symbol for mouth-sound

to let u know how my peepl died (every dae)

u can-not noe   (this : tha edge of unselfing)   un-less u know how to reed
plane bone

tha continuum crackin open // of dead hips out-side pressure is always app-lied

where my peepl have gone   in tha back of thr heds   insyd tha insyd
tha t   reel heart cave   beyond tha   t

u   uuuu   can-not   f a l l   o   it is nt for carnal flesh

thr is no use for tha ear

breath

has no out-side-side

if u wnt to come in   yull hv to dig a hole & sit in all dis drt (up too tha neck)
(wade in mthr) (a las(t))

tht nay-k-d-ness u wan-te-d   promisd   i gave u   thin deaths (day-lee) is
nthin moor than TRUth

uuuuuuu u flipt pasdt me   && still look-in

this cave of language (sayin nthin eternull)

tha moor u lrn too die tha gud way tha lss it hrts   fall wit ur back curld   em-
bree-on-ic   & u do nt reel-lee fall   wen u put dis / me / dwn thr wll
be not a sownd & tht is won type of gud death   this is me   led-in u go   do u
wnt to call tht benev(i)olense   do u wnt to call it at all

(ur sy-lense shall nt be mstkn fo death)

remoov-all   thn   u   rez rrrrrr e k t   it.

NOTES

we n' de ya ho

The italicized line in PART II is a slightly altered phrase from a 2015 *Slate* article entitled, "Why Do So Many Americans Think They Have Cherokee Blood?: The history of a myth."

una parda, which is me

The definition offered at the beginning of the poem is a compilation of information gathered while doing research on the term 'pardo.' The following scholarly articles inspired the explanation: "Spaniards, 'Pardos', and the Missing Mestizos: Identities and Racial Categories in the Early Hispanic Caribbean" by Stuart B. Schwartz, "The Use of Racial and Ethnic Terms in America: Management by Manipulation" by Jack D. Forbes (where some of the text is more directly used), the 1998 Second Edition of "Compilation of Colonial Spanish Terms and Document Related Phrases" written by Ophelia Marquez and Lillian Ramos Navarro Wold, and "Educational Inequality by Race in Brazil, 1982-2007: Structural Changes and Shifts in Racial Classification" by Leticia J. Marteleto.

ACT !   pose with fingers as though cigarette (puff puff)

The opening line alludes to the Shakespearean speech spoken by King Henry in *Henry V* (Act III Scene I), which begins with, "Once more unto the breach, dear friends, once more..." The line talking about the wild-haired virgin is referring to the John Patrick Shanley play, *Savage in Limbo*, and the lines about Clov are hinting towards a character by that same name in the Samuel Beckett one-act, *Endgame*.

I'M A BLACK BLACK BLACK BLACK BLACK BLACK TAN WOMAN

The second line of the third stanza riffs off a part of Lady Macbeth's monologue in *Macbeth* (Act V Scene I), where she exclaims, "Out, damned spot, out, I say!"

CoNTInenTAL

The opening stanza refers to Max Ritvo's "The Curve," in *Four Reincarnations*, as well as a dear friend of mine and their thoughts on the state of the rock star.

ACKNOWLEDGMENTS

My sincere gratitude to the editors of the following publications, where some of these poems first appeared:

American Chordata: "BELUGA," "desert room #3 (el rey court)";

The Brooklyn Review: "ACT !   pose with fingers as though cigarette (puff puff)";

Glass: A Journal of Poetry: "FIERCER STILL, FIERCER YET";

Lampblack: "I TOO WANT TO EAT THE WORLD";

PANK: "una parda, which is me";

Pigeon Pages: "all the matriarchs in spain are dead";

Poetry Northwest: "we n' de ya ho," "MAMI : a chest for healing."

Heartfelt thanks to my forever sweets: Baba, Mami, Papi, Ananda, my family down south and in Spain, abuelo, abuelita, Nana, Papa, Uncle Billy, Aunt Thelma, Big Mother (Lena!!!), Big Daddy, and all my ancestors. Thank you for the eternal love and protection you all offer me, for showing up in my dreams, for having shown up in my childhood and now my adulthood, and for keeping me strong always and in all ways.

A massive thank you to all the teachers and classmates (literary and otherwise) I learned from and was pushed by throughout my schooling. Shoutout to Dorla McIntosh, for making the undergraduate creative writing department at Columbia feel like home, for all the down-to-earth conversations we had in your office, and for taking care of so many budding writers. To Timothy Donnelly, for being such an exuberant, hilarious, and downright knowledgeable source of literary information; I especially appreciate you for allowing me to be quiet during workshop, as I carefully learned how to analyze poems. What a true kindness that is! To the late Marni Ludwig, for being a true badass with the biggest heart; I took your workshop two times because learning from you felt so right. Thank you for being so open, so understanding, so human. To Sharon Olds, for being the most gracious soul I've ever met. I will never forget our moments spent birdwatching in your office, or when you offered me some of your potato chips before delving into my poetry. Thank you. To Terrance Hayes, for gifting me the creative and intellectual space to explore any and all facets of my voice, and for taking the time to see what I was up to on the page so I could in turn get a better sense of where I was heading artistically. I can never forget my two English teachers in high school, Richard, for reading poems like they were the most delicious monologues, and Paul K., for having such exceptional taste in literature. What a dream it was to learn from such masters and have my adolescent brain engage with brilliant books that still occupy many of my thoughts today.

To BOA: Muchísimas gracias a Aracelis Girmay for being such a generous and openminded reader of my manuscript and for being willing to take a chance on something so, well, wild. I remain humbled to have such a beautiful platform for my work, and that is all because of you. My absolute appreciation to the team at BOA for providing a true home full of kindness, understanding, and dedication to seeing your writers' visions through. Thank you as well to Sandy for such an exquisitely abstract cover design. You knew exactly which visual elements to represent my words with, and for that I am grateful.

Thank you, dear reader(s), for giving me a moment of your time. What a pleasure it is to be seen/read/heard out.

ABOUT THE AUTHOR

India Lena González is a poet, editor, and multidisciplinary artist. She received her BA from Columbia University, where she graduated with honors, and her MFA from New York University's Creative Writing Program. While at NYU she served as a writing instructor for undergraduates and received a Writers in the Public Schools fellowship enabling her to teach literature to middle school students via Teachers & Writers Collaborative. India is also a professionally trained dancer, choreographer, and actor. She is the features editor of *Poets & Writers Magazine* and lives in Harlem.

BOA Editions, Ltd.
A. Poulin, Jr. New Poets of America Series

No. 1 *Cedarhome*
Poems by Barton Sutter
Foreword by W. D. Snodgrass

No. 2 *Beast Is a Wolf with Brown Fire*
Poems by Barry Wallenstein
Foreword by M. L. Rosenthal

No. 3 *Along the Dark Shore*
Poems by Edward Byrne
Foreword by John Ashbery

No. 4 *Anchor Dragging*
Poems by Anthony Piccione
Foreword by Archibald MacLeish

No. 5 *Eggs in the Lake*
Poems by Daniela Gioseffi
Foreword by John Logan

No. 6 *Moving the House*
Poems by Ingrid Wendt
Foreword by William Stafford

No. 7 *Whomp and Moonshiver*
Poems by Thomas Whitbread
Foreword by Richard Wilbur

No. 8 *Where We Live*
Poems by Peter Makuck
Foreword by Louis Simpson

No. 9 *Rose*
Poems by Li-Young Lee
Foreword by Gerald Stern

No. 10 *Genesis*
Poems by Emanuel di Pasquale
Foreword by X. J. Kennedy

No. 11 *Borders*
Poems by Mary Crow
Foreword by David Ignatow

No. 12 *Awake*
Poems by Dorianne Laux
Foreword by Philip Levine

No. 13 *Hurricane Walk*
Poems by Diann Blakely Shoaf
Foreword by William Matthews

No. 14 *The Philosopher's Club*
Poems by Kim Addonizio
Foreword by Gerald Stern

No. 15 *Bell 8*
Poems by Rick Lyon
Foreword by C. K. Williams

No. 16 *Bruise Theory*
Poems by Natalie Kenvin
Foreword by Carolyn Forché

No. 17 *Shattering Air*
Poems by David Biespiel
Foreword by Stanley Plumly

No. 18 *The Hour Between Dog and Wolf*
Poems by Laure-Anne Bosselaar
Foreword by Charles Simic

No. 19 *News of Home*
Poems by Debra Kang Dean
Foreword by Colette Inez

No. 20 *Meteorology*
Poems by Alpay Ulku
Foreword by Yusef Komunyakaa

No. 21 *The Daughters of Discordia*
Poems by Suzanne Owens
Foreword by Denise Duhamel

No. 22 *Rare Earths*
Poems by Deena Linett
Foreword by Molly Peacock

No. 23 *An Unkindness of Ravens*
Poems by Meg Kearney
Foreword by Donald Hall

No. 24 *Hunting Down the Monk*
Poems by Adrie Kusserow
Foreword by Karen Swenson

COLOPHON

BOA Editions, Ltd., a not-for-profit publisher of poetry and other literary works, fosters readership and appreciation of contemporary literature. By identifying, cultivating, and publishing both new and established poets and selecting authors of unique literary talent, BOA brings high-quality literature to the public.

Support for this effort comes from the sale of its publications, grant funding, and private donations.

*

The publication of this book is made possible, in part, by the special support of the following individuals:

Anonymous
Angela Bonazinga & Catherine Lewis
Christopher C. Dahl
James Long Hale
Margaret B. Heminway
Charles Hertrick & Joan Gerrity
Nora A. Jones
Keetje & Sarah Kuipers
Paul LaFerriere & Dorrie Parini, *in honor of Bill Waddell*
Jack & Gail Langerak
Barbara Lovenheim
Richard Margolis & Sherry Phillips
Joe McElveney
Daniel M. Meyers, *in honor of J. Shepard Skiff*
The Mountain Family, *in support of poets & poetry*
Nocon & Associates
Boo Poulin
John H. Schultz
Robert Thomas
William Waddell & Linda Rubel
Michael Waters & Mihaela Moscaliuc
Bruce & Jean Weigl